Tracy Woodsford

Hands-on Bible Creativity

25 activities for
groups to bring the
Bible to life

This book is dedicated to Woody, who allows me the freedom to pursue even the wildest of my dreams...

and to Lydia, who always wants to help me with my 'art stuff'

My thanks go to Dean for asking the question...

Also to Stewart and Carol Henderson for their insight and very helpful feedback

© Tracy Woodsford 2004

First published 2004
ISBN 1 84427 081 5

Scripture Union, 207-209 Queensway, Bletchley, Milton Keynes, MK2 2EB, England
Email: info@scriptureunion.org.uk
Website: www.scriptureunion.org.uk

Scripture Union Australia: Locked Bag 2, Central Coast Business Centre, NSW 2252 www.su.org.au

Scripture Union USA: PO Box 987, Valley Forge, PA 19482, USA www.scriptureunion.org

Unless otherwise stated, Scripture quotations are from the Holy Bible, New International Version. Copyright © 1973, 1978, 1984 by International Bible Society. Anglicisation copyright © 1979, 1984, 1989. Used by permission of Hodder and Stoughton Ltd.

British Library Cataloguing in Publication Data.
A catalogue record of this book is available from the British Library.

Cover design by David Lund Design and Advertising Ltd
Internal design and layout by Servis Filmsetting Ltd, Manchester
Illustrations by Wendy Hobbs
Printed and bound by Interprint Ltd, Malta

Scripture Union is an international Christian charity working with churches in more than 130 countries providing resources to bring the good news about Jesus Christ to children, young people and families – and to encourage them to develop spiritually through the Bible and prayer.

As well as our network of volunteers, staff and associates who run holidays, church-based events and school Christian groups, we produce a wide range of publications and support those who use our resources through training programmes.

Foreword

We have known Tracy for some years, and her creativity has always impressed us. In particular, we have been struck by the way she uses her considerable gifts to reveal the hidden wonders of a life spent walking with God. Tracy also challenges us, through her work, to reflect on the exuberant conclusion of our own pilgrimage – the entry into 'the further place, the final home, the treasury of joy'.

Having spent a lot of time in hospital over the years, Carol has loved the way Tracy's designs can truly lift an individual out of a suffering present and show a bigger picture with its inherent glorious truths. And, typical of Tracy's servant heart is the way she has designed this book to animate both the enjoyment and the glory of making beautiful things meld with the inspirational topics and challenges of her biblical themes.

We love her work. We know that individuals and groups will be both blessed and inspired by following the helpful guidelines in the rich pages of *Hands-on Bible Creativity*. Her designs really are accessible – even to those of us less talented – and we guarantee a lot of fun in the process!

Being passionate about 'wholeness' in every part of our lives as a reflection of our glorious, wholly great God, we cannot recommend *Hands-on Bible Creativity* too highly, as it combines practical activity with spiritual insight, depth and growth.

Carol and Stewart Henderson

Carol and Stewart Henderson have a passion for Christ and seek to spread the gospel through creative arts, in particular poetry and the spoken word. Stewart has read his poetry on all five BBC stations. Carol is, among other things, a Myers-Briggs practitioner, helping others to find their best way of working in the kingdom of God.

What they said about Hands-on Bible Creativity . . .

Hands-on Bible Creativity provides activities for use in a whole variety of group settings: adult small groups, youth groups, with Christians and seekers, women's groups, church weekends away. . . Here's what some different group leaders have said about it:

Mike North co-ordinates the youth and children's work at St Michael le Belfrey, York. Young people and children come from all around York to the mid-week clubs which are cell-based. Relationships are key to the work, and activities that can be completed together are key to relationship building.

Mike says, 'I love the way the book is ordered; offering suggested age groups, timings and Bible references with easy-to-follow instructions that even I can understand! Some of the activities suggest ways of taking the ideas further and "stepping outside the box". A great resource for leaders that shows what is attainable through creativity.'

Mike Law runs the Christian Resources Project, trains small group leaders and children's workers and is the author of *Small Groups Growing Churches.*

'As someone who, in Tracy's words, has "not fared well under art teachers" I approached this book with trepidation. There was no need. The instructions are clear, the projects varied and the whole book an inspiration for even the artistically challenged to bring some creativity into our understanding of the Bible and ourselves. An excellent alternative to the traditional small group study, which will also be valuable in all-age activities.'

Claire Torrens works with the over-sixties in St Luke's Church, Maidstone, Kent. They are a very mixed group varying in Christian belief and commitment.

Claire says, 'Recently we have begun to help them discover their creativity and ultimately more about themselves, something the majority have never had much opportunity to do. ... *Hands-on Bible Creativity* opens up the Bible and provides a course of potential discovery, fun and adventure. I think this will have the ability to open long-shut doors that formal teaching would not reach with this group. The way it has been set out is clear and uncomplicated and we look forward to using it.'

Contents

Introduction

When my good friend Dean asked me when I was going to write my book, I asked him what he was talking about. I had had ideas about possibly starting an art magazine, but writing a book had not crossed my mind. He said Christians needed something to help them grasp hold of God's Word in a creative way and perhaps I could come up with something that would help in that area.

I find it sad that, in a world saturated with visual images – billboards, TV advertisements, magazines, films, paintings, installations, visual art of all descriptions – Christians seem very tentative about visual and tactile creativity. I have always been annoyed when, at conferences and suchlike, I have seen advertisements for seminars that purport to be about the arts but only include drama, dance and music. There is nothing wrong with these aspects of artistry, but where are all the *visual* arts? Where is the painting? Where are the ceramics and the fabric art?

We seem to have lost sight of our God as Creator. The first thing we read about God doing, in Genesis 1, is creating. All three persons of the Trinity are there, working together, bringing everything into being, and we are made in God's image:

'Then God said, "Let us make man in our image, after our likeness"' (Genesis 1:26RSV).

There is, of course, an important distinction between God the Creator and us as creative people, in that he created from nothing! However, using the things which God provides – our gifts, learned skills, imagination, and all sorts of materials – we *can* create things of beauty and practicality, using his creation as inspiration. Who can look at a tree, flower, leaf, insect or shell and not marvel at their infinite variety? They could all have been made exactly the same as each other, but the God we love is a God who is creative. Having been made in his image we, too, have the ability to make beautiful things which challenge and stimulate awe and worship of our Creator, whether we have found our artistic niche or not.

In Exodus 35:30 – 36:2 we read about Bezalel being commissioned to make articles for the tabernacle. It says in verses 31-33:
'...he has filled him with the Spirit of God, with ability, with intelligence, with knowledge and with all craftsmanship, to devise artistic designs, to work in gold and silver and bronze, in cutting stones for setting, and in carving wood, for work in every skilled craft' (RSV).

God could have had his tabernacle made of plain, though luxurious, materials, but he chose to have it designed with beautiful patterns and skilful embroidery. We are told that God gave his craftsmen knowledge and skill in how to design (verses 32 and 35). Notice, too, that God said that he wanted cherubim depicted in the tabernacle curtains but there seems to have been freedom in exactly how that was done. There were guidelines inside of which there was freedom, and the imagery all around worshippers in the tabernacle would have reminded them of God.

As well as stimulating us to worship, the creative process and the results of it are all visual aids to our understanding and reinforcers for our memories. Think of the stained glass windows in some of our churches, the pictures in our children's Bibles, banners and patterned kneelers. What we hear, what we see and what we do combine to help us understand better and learn more quickly. We can learn about God through reading the Bible, but it is not until we engage with it more practically and live it, that our understanding of, and relationship with, God grow. In much the same way we can read a set of instructions and learn something about how an item is put together, but following those instructions and actually making the product gives us much better insight, and the task is filed away in our memories more clearly.

When our children bring us something that they have made, we are delighted, and praise their efforts. We place their finger paintings where they can be seen by others because we are proud of them. In the same way, God delights in our fumbling efforts to emulate him in artistry. I pray that, in following these projects, you may have a better understanding of God and the Bible through the process of creating.

For those who are unsure...

When dealing with people who are unsure about art and creativity, remember to be gentle, and encouraging! Some of us have not fared well under art teachers, or have been ridiculed by others, sometimes unintentionally. Here are a few pointers which might help the nervous to venture out of their shells and have a go.

1 We must stress that these projects, and any other artistic endeavours are between us and our Maker. They are not for display in a gallery. They are purely personal.
2 Don't force people to show what they have made to the rest of the group. Those who want to share will do so.
3 Emphasise the idea that it is not the end product or what anyone else thinks of the end product that is most important, but the process – that we have engaged in an activity that is pleasing to God in an endeavour to learn more about him.
4 Remember that praise works wonders. We praise our children's efforts when they first step out into anything new and in doing so, we give them confidence to try other, more difficult things.

How to use this resource

I want this book to be useful to all sorts of groups – mature Christians, seekers, new believers, male and female, young or not so young. So many practical and artistic resources are seen as being useful for youth and children's work but when we reach adulthood, there seems to be very little available for us to engage with in an imaginative and tactile way.

Not all of these projects will be useful to every group, but you will find something here to suit the whole variety of group contexts including mother and toddler groups, elderly friendship groups, house groups, prayer groups, youth groups, seeker groups, weekends away, and so on: anywhere people are gathering together to learn more about Jesus.

Some of the projects could be achieved in a 'whole church' setting, while others work better with smaller groups. I have tried to give an idea of how long a project might take, although obviously, that is flexible, depending on the amount of decoration individuals use … and how much talking goes on! Try out each project yourself beforehand, so that you can anticipate and help with any problems the group encounters. Use the introduction and the Bible passages suggested as a starting point for the group to explore as fully as they want to. They are by no means exhaustive. Keep a concordance handy so that people may look up other appropriate passages. Do use the Bible and theme index to help you find other relevant activities.

Some ideas for using *Hands-on Bible Creativity*

1. With non-Christians
   • Doing something while talking about the Bible is a non-threatening way of introducing seekers to who God is, and what he requires of us. It allows those who are naturally quiet to remain so, without feeling conspicuous. It is less 'confrontational'. It allows room for friendship to develop as everybody learns together and helps each other along; it creates a more relaxed atmosphere than a question and answer session.
   • A short presentation of the subject could be given while everybody has a drink at the beginning, allowing for questions and conversation to occur while you're creating. Mixing Christians and seekers works well, allowing the sharing of questions and answers, and giving opportunity for several viewpoints and illustrations.
   • These projects work best with people already interested in crafts, so that they are not faced with worries about their creative abilities. Such concerns would add to any tension caused by the need to work out what Christianity is all about.
   • You could choose six projects to work on over six weeks. For example, you might like to start with 'Community' and work through 'God's character', 'Obedience', 'Repentance', 'Adoption', finishing with 'Reconciliation' and a challenge to respond.

2. In-depth study
These projects are also ideal for more established groups who want to go deeper with Bible passages or themes. Many of the subjects covered in this book could be discussed over a long period. For example, pick out 12 projects and study one a month. Discuss the theme for a couple of sessions, then enjoy the craft.

3. The 'mystery' angle

Why not have your group tackle the project without telling them what it is about? At the end, ask them what they think the subject is. This can be fun, as several of the projects can work for different subjects if looked at in different ways.

4 Just dip in

Perhaps you are just looking for something different to do as part of an existing group or for a church event or weekend away? If you are studying a passage or theme, check out the Bible and theme index at the back of this book and find a suitable appropriate craft for the age range and group size.

Materials

Most of these projects use readily available and inexpensive materials, and several call for decorative paper. I decorate my own paper, but realise that there may not be time for people to do this during group sessions. If you intend to follow many of the projects, you might want to spend a session at the beginning making your own papers for use later, so here are a few different techniques. They are simple and help to knit together members of a new group or a group in which there are people anxious about doing anything 'arty'.

If you don't want to decorate your own paper, it is easy to build up a paper supply without too much trouble. Wrapping paper, foil and cellophane wrappings from chocolate and sweets, and colourful pages in magazines are easily picked up. Start collecting any paper which catches your eye so that you have a supply ready for your group. Remember, there will be those in the group who don't feel very confident 'doing art', but having a box of lovely materials may just set them off on a journey of inspiration.

Commonly used materials for your supply:
• different types of paper – tissue, gummed, metallic, plain, patterned
• thin (approx 200 gsm) and thick card (approx 230 gsm)
• pens: gel, metallic, OHP, markers, felt-tips
• paints and inks
• PVA glue
• glue spreaders
• A4 paper
• scrap paper for designing
• scissors

If you can't find the materials you need in an art or stationery shop, most can be bought mail order from: Craft Creations Ltd, Ingersoll House, Delamare Road, Cheshunt, Herts, EN8 9HD, 01992 781900, www.craftcreations.co.uk. Alternatively, check out www.uk.opitec.com.

Five ways to decorate paper

1 Fill an old plant spray bottle with paint or ink and spray it on white or coloured paper. Try with a single colour or several colours; with stripes masked off with masking tape or with a stencil. Experiment.
2 Mix some wallpaper paste and put small amounts in yogurt or margarine pots. Mix poster paints with the paste, different colours in each pot. Using a wide paint brush (about 3 cm), spread some coloured paste on a sheet of paper and place another sheet on top. Press down then peel the pieces apart. Because the paste is thick and sticky, it leaves peaks of deeper colour which give interesting patterns. You should now have mirror image patterns. Use one or more colours together, make stripes, swirls, squares – use your imagination.
3 Squirt some paint on an old plate and dip a sponge in it. Sponge the paint on to paper. Use different shapes and sizes of sponge, as well as a mix of colours.
4 Take a metallic pen for a walk. Start in one corner of the paper and squiggle across the page in random loops. This is particularly effective on dark/black paper.
5 Place a piece of A4 paper in a shallow tray. Dip a marble into some paint and place in the tray, and move the tray so that the marble rolls around randomly over the paper.

That should start you off. If your group decides to do this together, make sure that you have a lot of space to let everything dry, as paper decoration can be addictive. Before you know it, you'll have a ream of patterned paper all over the floor, and you won't be able to get to the door!

A few tips before you begin . . .

There are a few things that might be helpful for several activities so we've listed them here rather than repeating them in the instructions for each project.

To score and fold card
Use an old ball point pen which no longer works and press hard along the line to be folded. Make sure you do this on what will be the *inside* of the fold. The card should now fold easily. Alternatively, line up a metal ruler with the fold line, and bend the card over the ruler to get a straight edge. To sharpen the crease, run the bowl of a teaspoon over it.

For decorative lettering
If any group member does not feel confident about calligraphy, you could print several sheets of different fonts from a computer, or pick out interesting lettering from old magazines. Use pens with chisel-shaped nibs and you will automatically produce thick and thin strokes as you write.

For poetry writing
Have a thesaurus to hand to avoid repetition. It also helps when you have a sense of what you want to say but not the words to say it. A dictionary of rhyming words can be helpful, as can a concordance, to help you find what the Bible says about your subject.

Sticking
Double-sided sticky tape is useful if you haven't time for glue to dry.

Glue spreaders
You can buy plastic glue spreaders, but the straight side of a scrap of thick card works just as well.

Cleaning up
Make sure you use the correct cleaning fluid to clean brushes. Glass paints, for example, are not usually water-soluble and need to be cleaned with white spirit.

Important note: before using paints, dyes, glues, etc, always read the directions on the packet to make sure they are suitable for the project and so that you can take any necessary safety precautions.

Worship

Logistics

Time – 60 minutes; Age – 10 years up; Group – up to 20

Bible link

Exodus 20:3–6; 2 Kings 17:35,36; 1 Chronicles 16:29; Daniel 3; John 4:21–24; Romans 12:1,2; Revelation 4:1–11

Introduction

Did you know that there are several words translated 'worship' in the New Testament?

1. *Proskuneo* – to bow down to kiss; to make obeisance; do reverence to; to serve.
2. *Sebomai* – to revere, stressing the feeling of awe or devotion.
3. *Latreuo* – to serve (especially divine service, as in Israel's worship).
4. *Eusebeo* – to act piously towards.

This project consists of making a representation of a stained glass window to place somewhere in the home or workspace as a visual reminder that we should worship God always and everywhere. Worship isn't something which only happens in a particular place at a particular time (see John 4:21–24); it is an attitude of heart towards a God worthy of our praise.

You will need

Black paper and coloured gummed paper *or* acetate and acetate pens; PVA glue; glue spreaders; scrap paper and pencils; scissors, templates from pages 57–58

Method

Before beginning, read the lovely poem on page 12 to your group to inspire them. It is reproduced here with the author's permission.

1. First of all, everybody needs to decide which shape to use for their design – square, rectangular, circular, arch, triptych, diamond. Templates are provided on pages 57–58. Enlarge the template to your preferred size. Copy this onto scrap paper, by either tracing or drawing around the template.

2. Think of a design for your window. Remember to allow fairly thick outlines for the 'leading'. This doesn't have to be wildly artistic. In fact, simple abstract shapes can look extremely effective, as black outlines and bright colours are very dramatic.

3. Decide on your method – either:
   - acetates and acetate pens to provide the 'glass', with black paper for the border.
   - black paper background with gummed paper as the 'glass'.

If you are using acetate, place a sheet of clear acetate over your design and copy in the black lines. Now colour in the spaces with acetate pens or glass paint. Once this is completed, cut a black paper frame and stick it to the acetate. This looks good hanging in a window where the light can shine through it.

If you are using a black paper background, lightly mark in pencil the shape of your chosen design and make a copy before cutting out the pieces so that when you come to stick them down, it is easier to tell which is which. Cut out one design from scrap paper and use the pieces as templates. Draw round the pieces on the gummed side of the coloured paper so that your pencil marks don't show on the right side. You must remember to turn all the templates over when doing this, otherwise you will end up with mirror images of your design – a problem if you are using lettering. Stick the coloured paper pieces inside the marked shape. Remember to leave gaps between them for the black paper to show through so that it looks like the window leading.

Alternative idea

Coloured tissue stuck behind the empty window cut-outs of your window frame is also highly effective when hung in front of the light. However, this is rather fiddly as you will need a craft knife to cut out the little sections of window.

How To Build A Sanctuary

How to build a sanctuary?
With fire doors and stellar fountains,
dormer windows, and a ski slope
beside Artex-splattered mountains.

How to build a sanctuary?
In technicoloured pastel,
where pensioners can join the crèche
then hog the Bouncy Castle.

How to build a sanctuary?
Fulfil the regulations
with an altar made of butterflies
where death meets celebration.

How to build a sanctuary?
Where lions lie down with lambs
and buttresses can really fly —
off searching for the damned.

How to build a sanctuary?
Without regard to cost,
an overflowing temple
for the worthless and the lost.

How to build a sanctuary?
With brass embroidered dome
where the blind see birds of paradise
and the homeless find their home.

Obedience

Logistics

Time – 30 minutes; Age – any; Group – no size limit

Bible link

Exodus 19:4–6; Deuteronomy 6:1–3; 11:26–28; Matthew 7:21–23; John 14:21–24; Romans 5:18,19; 6:16–18; 1 Peter 1:22–25; 2 John 1:5,6

Introduction

Obedience – the willing submission to another's rule; compliance.

Do we jump at the chance to do as we have been commanded? Or are we scared of taking risks? Is there a limit to the price we are willing to pay to be obedient in all things? If there is, why is that? Sometimes it is easier to do the big things and neglect those smaller, seemingly insignificant tasks. But if God is asking, does that not become significant? If something is important enough for the Lord of the universe to take an interest in it, should it not also be important enough for us to sit up and take notice?

You will need

Pens; scrap paper; dictionary; thesaurus; rhyming dictionary (optional)

Method

1. You might want to ask the group some of the questions posed in the introduction and look at some of the passages listed above and other passages to do with obedience. What strikes you or challenges you from these? Write a poem on any aspect of obedience. Remember, this is personal. If people are happy to read out their poems, that's fine, but their words are between them and God. As such, those words are special, even if the writer doesn't rate him/herself highly as a poet. The main thing is to express something of his/her feelings about obedience, not to write prize-winning poetry.

2. Begin by asking each group member to write a short list of words associated with obedience. This should give some idea of the flavour and direction of the poem, and also helps to get over the blank page/sheer panic syndrome.

3. Once this is done, flesh out the poem. Remember, it doesn't have to be long. It doesn't have to rhyme. Humorous or serious, it doesn't matter. Just write.

Obedience

Obedience costs, for it asks of me
Those things that are beyond me.
When my spirit talks
Of doing things
I do not want to do,
I know it's You.
I am small and weak
And do not want to show
My vulnerability
By sticking out my neck.
But when the call is strong
My spirit stirs me up.
I fight against the fear of risk
Then yield to Your wishes
And see the reaping
Of a treasure I could not imagine.
When You ask me to give
Of myself
And take that extra step
I grow when I see
That You carry me.

© Tracy Woodsford

No compromise

Logistics

Time – 30 minutes; Age – any; Group – no size limit

Bible link

The sinful nature: Matthew 18: 7–9; Romans 8:5–9; Galatians 5:16–21
Stone markers: Genesis 28:18–22; 31:45–49; Joshua 4:1–7

Introduction

With God there must be no compromise. However, there are still areas in our lives where we like to fudge the issue a bit, trying to justify ourselves – 'Well, I'm not as bad as so-and-so'. We don't want to let go of some of our sins, trying any devious means to hold on to them. Who are we trying to fool?

There are several passages in the Bible where people set up a monument of stones. Sometimes those stones acted as a visual reminder that God met them there (Genesis 28:18–22) and sometimes, in addition, they acted as a boundary marker, to say 'This far and no further.' (Genesis 31:45–49). About which issues in your life do you need to say 'This far and no further. I will no longer compromise on this.'?

You might like to look at the stones as cairns, or memorials, marking the death of a particular sin – 'I will no longer...' or 'I am not going to compromise my faith on...'

You will need

12 stones per person; a camera – ideally digital or Polaroid; pens

Method

The ideal situation would be to visit a beach with an unlimited supply of stones, and everyone can pick out twelve. However, if this is not possible, visit your local garden centre, or have each person provide stones from their gardens.

1. Ask everyone in the group to think and pray about what their sculpture will represent for them – which sin are they going to give up? Where will they place the boundary on compromise? They needn't share this, as long as each person knows what they are saying before God.

2. Once this has been decided, arrange the stones in a pleasing manner. If possible, borrow a copy of Andy Goldsworthy's book *Stone* to give people ideas. Photograph each sculpture. Each group member can write on the back of their picture what the sculpture represents for them.

Alternative ideas

Why not use this project to look at the subject of God's provision. When land was given out, boundary stones showed what belonged to whom. Moses particularly instructed the people not to move these stones (Deuteronomy 27:17). When people moved boundary stones, they were saying that God's provision was not enough for them. Your stone sculptures can represent that God's provision is enough for you.

The character of God

Logistics

Time – 60 minutes; Age – 10 years up; Group – up to 30

Bible link

Here is the list of words I used, with references, in case you have trouble finding characteristics for some of the letters.

Awesome – Deuteronomy 7:21; 28:58, Psalm 68:35
Beautiful – Psalm 27:4
Creative – Genesis 1
Divine – Romans 1:20; 2 Peter 1:3,4
Enabling – Luke 1:74; Acts 2:4; 14:3
Faithful – Deuteronomy 7:9; Isaiah 49:7; 1 Corinthians 10:13
Gracious – Nehemiah 9:31; Psalm 111:4; Joel 2:13
Holy – Leviticus 11:44; Luke 1:49; 1 Peter 1:15,16
Immortal – Romans 1:23; 1 Timothy 1:17; 6:16
Jealous – Exodus 20:5; Deuteronomy 4:24; Ezekiel 5:13
Kind – Psalm 145:17; Isaiah 63:7; Luke 6:35
Loving – Deuteronomy 23:5; Psalm 25:10; 1 John 4:8
Merciful – Deuteronomy 4:31; Nehemiah 9:31; Daniel 9:9
Noble – James 2:7
Omniscient – 2 Chronicles 6:30; Psalm 139
Perfect – Deuteronomy 32:4; 2 Samuel 22:31; Matthew 5:48
Quietening – Zephaniah 3:17; Mark 4:39; Luke 4:35
Righteous – Ezra 9:15; Psalm 4:1; Acts 3:14
Sinless – 2 Corinthians 5:21; Hebrews 4:15
Trustworthy – 2 Samuel 7:28; Psalm 19:7
Understanding – Psalm 147:5,
Victorious – John 16:33; Revelation 17:14
Wise – Job 9:4; Psalm 104:24; Ephesians 3:10
Yahweh – God's name tells you what he is like – 'I am' Exodus 3:14
Zealous – 2 Kings 19:31; Isaiah 26:11; Ezekiel 5:13

Introduction

This project is designed to help you reflect on what God is like. Why is it good to think more deeply about the characteristics of God? There are lots of reasons: where possible we are encouraged to emulate our Father, showing to others the same impartiality and grace he shows us, and you can't emulate someone you don't know. The more we find out about God, the more we are challenged to evaluate our own attitudes and behaviour in the light of God's perfect standard, and to value the qualities in each other that reflect him. But some of the characteristics of God are unique to him and the main reason for finding out more about God is so that we can worship him better. This project should provide you with lots of fuel for reflection and worship.

You will need

Paper for the completed alphabet; scrap paper – several sheets for each person; pens – gel, metallic, felt-tips etc; sheets of letters in different fonts, or pages from magazines; PVA glue; glue spreaders

Method

1. Write the alphabet down the left-hand side of a piece of paper. Write one of God's qualities for each letter, preferably with at least one reference to back it up. It would be handy to have a concordance available as although we may think we know about God's character, it is helpful to be able to back up our assertions. Alternatively you could hand out a psalm such as Psalm 103, which is full of statements about God, to act as a springboard for people's ideas.

2. Once you have your list of qualities – you will probably need to confer to fill in the more awkward letters – you need some scrap paper to sketch out an arrangement of those words. Please assure your group not to worry about perfection. This is for *them*, not to hang in a gallery for all to see. If they want to line up all the words down the left hand side of the page, then that is as valid as any other arrangement. If they don't want the alphabet in order, that's fine. There are no rules of presentation. The object is to reflect on the character of God, and on how that affects us.

3. When you are happy with your arrangement, take a piece of paper (patterned, plain, white, coloured, whatever you want for the finished article) and either write out your selected words, or cut up some printed pages of fonts and stick on the letters.

An alphabet showing some of God's qualities

Alternative idea

As an additional exercise, each person could write out the alphabet again, putting his own name at the top. These pieces of paper can then be passed around the group, and each person can fill in a few of the letters with qualities that the named person shows. At the end of the session, each group member would then have a sheet listing some of their godly characteristics. This should serve to build up individuals in the group, while also pointing out what God is like, and how much further we have to go to be like him.

Reconciliation

Logistics

Time – 60 minutes; Age – 10 years up; Group – up to 30

Bible link

Romans 5:9–11; Ephesians 2:13–16; Colossians 1:19,20; Hebrews 2:17; 9:11–14; Revelation 19:6–9

Introduction

The Greek word for reconciliation refers to the re-establishing of friendly interpersonal relations after a disruption or breakdown in the relationship. In the case of a Christian, our alienation from God as a result of sin is replaced by a relationship with him as Father, achieved through Jesus' death on the cross and our acceptance of him as Lord and Saviour.

The Bible uses the wonderful picture of a wedding feast to symbolise the totally restored, intimate and permanent relationship Jesus will one day have with his church – us! (see Revelation 19:6–9). All those who make Jesus their Lord are invited to this Wedding Feast. The box in this project is folded from a cruciform shape to remind us of the sacrifice that has brought about our reconciliation to God. The confetti in the box reminds us that we are invited to the wedding feast of the Lamb because of his atoning sacrifice for us.

You will need

Thin card; PVA glue; glue spreaders; scissors; pens – gel, metallic, markers etc; decorative hole punches, or confetti; coloured paper; template from page 59; patterned paper, tissue paper, stickers, sequins, anything you wish to use to embellish the box (optional)

Method

Preparation – photocopy the template provided onto the card, one for each member of your group.

1. Cut out the box shape from the card. You could do this beforehand, or ask each individual to do their own during the session.

2. Now you need to think about how the box will be decorated. If you wish to use patterned paper, glue the cut-out box template to the wrong side of the paper, then cut around the edge. If you do this, make sure you use very thin card for the box so that the paper does not tear when you fold the box. If you want to write on the box, or decorate it with paint or pen, this is more easily done before the box is folded.

3. Once the outside of the box is decorated to your satisfaction, score the lines on the template, ready to fold in to make a box shape. If you want to decorate the inside of the box, too, do not glue the box yet.

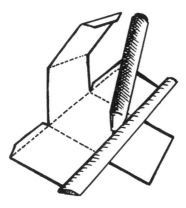

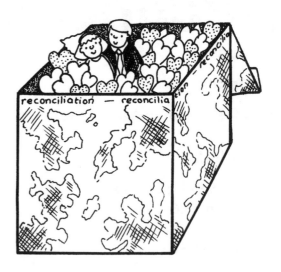

4. To decorate the inside of the box, you could line it with tissue paper of a different or complementary colour. Glue the box shape to the tissue paper then trim the edges.

5. Now fold the card into a box, and glue tabs A–D in place so that they will be inside the box. The other tab forms part of the lid and should not be glued.

6. When the box is dry, fill it with confetti. You can make your own confetti, using decorative hole punches in suitable shapes such as hearts or doves. If you have other wedding mementoes which will fit in the box, you could add those to remind you of the greater wedding feast to which we look forward.

The box may be made to different dimensions, but our sample size is large enough to hold several items, and not so small that it is fiddly for unsure fingers.

Alternative ideas

Use with other themes: atonement – sacrifice, propitiation, redemption.

You could also use this activity at Easter with the Good Friday project.

Why not put other things besides confetti in the box? You could use:

- Seeds – to symbolise the new life gained through the cross
- Tear-shaped cut-outs to remind us of the sadness of Good Friday
- Things for which you want to say 'sorry', written on small pieces of paper

Prayer

Logistics

Time – 45 minutes; Age – 10 years up; Group – up to 20

Bible link

Matthew 6:5–14; 26:36–44; Acts 1:14; 1 Timothy 2:1–4; Hebrews 7:25; James 5:13–18

Introduction

None of us feels we pray enough. There is always room for improvement and quite often we just don't know what to say. Sometimes we feel that there is no point in praying as nothing ever seems to change. But prayer is important, so important that Jesus, with his busy ministry, made sure that he took time to talk to his Father (Mark 1:35). Not only that, he taught us how to pray and gave us a prayer pattern (Matthew 6). He is still praying now, talking to God on our behalf (Hebrews 7:25).

This project sees us making a booklet containing the words of the Lord's Prayer. It can be easily carried around in a pocket or handbag, and used as a template for our prayers at any time. If you don't know what to say in prayer, start praying this prayer and see where it leads you. The journey will be different every time.

You will need

Thick card, or mount board (about 1 mm thick, available from art shops); decorative papers cut to 7 x 12.5 cm (see page 8 for instructions on how to decorate your own paper); PVA glue; glue spreaders; A4 paper; scissors; gel pens or felt-tip pens; scrap paper

Method

Preparation – cut the card or mounting board into 5 x 5 cm squares, two for each person. Each person will also need a strip of paper 4.5 x 27 cm.

1. Give each person two squares of card, a strip of paper, some scrap paper and some decorative paper, or the means to decorate some paper.

2. The paper strip needs to be folded into a concertina, so mark along its length every 4.5 cm, and fold it. This should make six squares.

3. On scrap paper, work out how you will divide up the verses of the Lord's Prayer into six sections, one to fit on each 4.5 cm square page.

4. To make the cover, glue the card squares on the decorative paper, leaving a gap of approximately 5 mm between them and about 10 mm all round. Carefully snip off the corners of the decorative paper. Fold in the 10 mm allowance, being especially careful with the corners, and glue the paper down. You have now made the cover for your booklet.

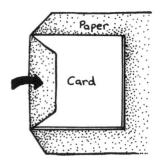

5. Lay the strip of paper inside the front cover so that all the folds of the concertina paper fall into the 'spine' of the book. Glue the left-hand end of the paper to the inside of the front cover. Now begin writing the Lord's Prayer. Use your imagination – illustrate; write in different colours; use different styles of writing. Remember, there are no right or wrong ways to do this.

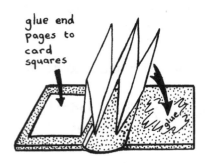

glue end
pages to
card
squares

6. When you have written the prayer, spread glue on the back of the last square and fix it to the right-hand inside cover. The inside 'pages' should open like a fan when the book is opened.

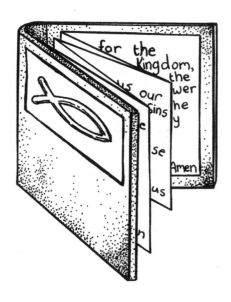

Praise

Logistics

Time – 30 minutes; Age – any; Group – no size limit

Bible link

Exodus 15:2; 1 Chronicles 16:23–25; Isaiah 25:1; Daniel 2:20–23; 1 Peter 1:3–7

Introduction

We are urged to praise God – to tell people about him; to make him known; to give him the glory and honour he deserves. The psalms are our starting point for this project, which consists of writing a psalm. As a starting point, why not print out copies of Psalm 8, 34, 89 or 147 for the group members? Praise springs naturally from love, so this project could also be used to look more deeply at that subject, concentrating on how we love God, how he loves us, and why.

You will need

Paper and pens

Method

1. This project is very simple. Study a few of the psalms. Note how they begin, progress, and end. What is their content? Where is the focus? What pattern do they follow? You'll find that many psalms involve a biography of the writer. They are written in specific situations and involve praise, thanksgiving and prayer.

2. Decide which pattern you want to follow, and where your emphasis will be. Jot down a few words or phrases you'd like to use.

3. Start writing!

4. You may want to write your psalm in calligraphy or type it up in a suitable font and place it somewhere you like to use for prayer. Perhaps you may want to keep it in a journal or somewhere more private. Use it during the day to praise God. Learn it, and sing it as a love song to our Lord and Saviour.

Praise

At Your footfall
The earth gives voice
Flowers bow down
The pebbles rejoice
Lightning sings a lullaby
Thunder hums the tune
The sun bobs a curtsey
Copied by the moon
Stars applaud ecstatically
Mountains bend the knee
Salty sea prostrates herself
With unremitting glee
Creation can't be silenced
In the presence of the King
I, too, am Your handiwork
My worship now I bring

© Tracy Woodsford

Community/family

Logistics

Time – 20 minutes; Age – 5 years up; Group – up to 30

Bible link

Joshua 22:13–20; Romans 12:3–8; 1 Corinthians 8:9–13; 12:12–26; Galatians 6:10; Ephesians 4:25; 1 Timothy 5:1,2; James 3:3–6; 1 Peter 2:17

Introduction

Community – a body of people living in one place and considered as a whole.
Family – all the descendants of a common ancestor.

In the Old Testament, the Jews are described as a community or congregation. They live together, follow the same rules for living, and are seen as a whole. If one member of the community sins, it affects others; sometimes all of them.

In the New Testament, believers are described as a family. Sometimes they are referred to as a body – a helpful image of interdependence. Again, the actions of an individual affect the whole group.

In this project, you are going to make a representation of this 'fabric' or 'body' by weaving paper to make a whole. Think about how, if any fibres in a piece of fabric break, a hole is quickly formed and the whole fabric starts to unravel. This is a good picture of how our actions can affect those around us.

You will need

A4 paper or thin coloured card; strips of paper of different colours and patterns; scissors or craft knives

Method

If you are working with young children or have a large group and not enough scissors, the slits can be cut in the A4 paper before the session.

1. In a sheet of A4 paper, make cuts which finish about 2 cm from the edge. These cuts may be straight or curved and do not need to be regular. However, they all need to be going in the same direction, either vertically or horizontally, and must be at least 1 cm apart to prevent tearing.

2. Weave strips of paper through the slits, alternating colours to produce a chequerboard effect. Use contrasting colours so that the pattern shows up well. Write around the edge of the paper: 'Now you are the body of Christ and each one of you is a part of it' (1 Corinthians 12:27).

Names

Logistics

Time – 45 minutes; Age – 5 years up; Group – up to 30

Bible link

For God's name's sake – Psalm 23:3; 25:11; 79:9; Isaiah 48:9; justified in God's name – 1 Corinthians 6:11; doing things in God's name – Colossians 3:17; James 5:14; calling on the name of the Lord – Genesis 26:25; Acts 2:21; 2 Timothy 2:19; baptised in the name – Matthew 28:19; Acts 19:5; Romans 6:3; God changes names – Genesis 17:5; 35:10; John 1:42; names in the book of life – Philippians 4:3; Revelation 20:15; God's name written on us – Revelation 3:12; 14:1

Introduction

You can't get away from names in the Bible. If it's not a list in Numbers, then it's God changing a person's name as a promise for the future. The names of God which we find in Scripture reflect aspects of his character. We are called to pray in the name of Jesus; call on his name; be baptised in his name. Names are important to God.

What does it mean to do something in someone's name? In biblical times, a person's name represented them; their character. It also carried their authority. This is why there is a commandment dealing solely with the use of the name of God. We must always honour God's reputation by speaking of him in a righteous way, and by not doing things which do not reflect his character.

This project involves making a simple collage incorporating one or more of the names of God which mean something special to us. Why not look up the meaning of your own name and put that in the collage, too?

You will need

Scrap paper; background paper; plain or decorative papers in a variety of colours; glue; a few copies of page 60; scissors; a concordance (optional); a book of names (optional)

Method

1. Decide which names to use (you might like to hand out copies of page 60 to get people started), then sketch the layout of your collage. Think about the use of colour – should you use many colours or just one in various shades? What colour will you use for the background? Think about the shape and conjunction of the shapes. Are there any relevant images suggested by the name(s)?

2. Select your coloured or decorative papers and draw the letters you need on the back. *Don't forget to draw them in reverse.* It is very annoying to cut out some fabulous letters and find they are all back-to-front when you come to stick them down!

3. Stick the background pieces on your base paper. Add the lettering and any other embellishments.

Alternative idea

These collages make good gifts for new babies and for baptisms.

Sanctification

Logistics

Time – 30 minutes; Age – teens up; Group – up to 20

Bible link

Matthew 5:48; Luke 6:36; Romans 8:29; 1 Corinthians 1:30,31; 6:11; 2 Corinthians 3:18; Galatians 5:22–26; Ephesians 5:1,2; 1 Peter 1:13–16; 2 Peter 3:18

Introduction

Sanctification – being made holy/set apart for God's use – is a status conferred on us the moment we become Christians, because of the sacrifice Jesus made for us on the cross. We are declared holy once and for all – set apart for God. But it is also an ongoing process of growing in holiness. We will never be perfect until Jesus' return, but as we mature as Christians and, with the transforming help of the Holy Spirit, fight against our sinful nature, we will become more and more Christlike.

This project involves dry-embossing a piece of paper. The paper is placed over a stencil, and pressure is applied until the pattern of the stencil can be seen in the paper. In much the same way, we want to carry the imprint of Jesus, and the more we, like the paper, are worked on by the Holy Spirit, the more of Christ can be seen in us.

You will need

Ready-made stencils (thick card or plastic) or card and craft knives; plain paper – white or coloured; scrap paper; pencils; old newspapers

Method

1. Sketch the pattern you wish to emboss. This could be a picture, shape, or words. Keep it simple, as you need to be able to cut it out easily.

2. Draw the pattern on the card and cut it out with a craft knife. Make sure you do this on a pad of newspaper or a cutting board to avoid unwanted cuts on the floor or table. Alternatively, use a ready-made stencil, available from craft shops or some DIY stores.

3. Place your chosen piece of paper over the stencil, remembering that if you are embossing words, the stencil must be in reverse. Now rub your fingertips carefully over the paper, applying a gentle pressure along the edges of the pattern.

4. Once the pattern is showing well, run the bowl of a teaspoon over the paper to sharpen the edges of the design.

Now remove the paper and turn it over. As you move the paper in the light, you should be able to see the pattern standing out.

5. Stick the paper carefully on a background paper of contrasting colour. Perhaps you might like to add a Bible verse which you have found particularly helpful or challenging.

Repentance

Logistics

Time – 90 minutes; Age – teens up; Group – up to 10

Bible link

Isaiah 59:20; Ezekiel 14:6; 18:30; Matthew 3:2,8; Luke 13:1–5; 15:7; Acts 3:19; 8:22; 11:18; 26:20; 2 Corinthians 7:9; 2 Peter 3:9; Revelation 9:21; 16:9

Introduction

Repentance is not only a profound regret over sin but, when accompanied by faith in Jesus Christ, results in a turning away from sin towards God and in an ongoing changed life. Repentance is not only necessary in the process of conversion but it is also a continuing attitude of heart in a disciple of Christ.

In this project, we will make a Jacob's ladder. It takes a turn of 180 degrees to send the blocks saying 'sin' tumbling over to say 'God'. This illustrates the fact that we have to turn completely in the opposite direction (180 degrees) from sin to find Christ. When you look at the ladder, you'll notice that 'sin' and 'God' cannot be seen at the same time. Sin is opposed to all the good things of God.

You will need

Per person: mounting card – 3 pieces 10 x 5 cm per person; thin ribbon, 0.5 cm wide – 6 pieces 13 cm long; decorative papers – 6 pieces 9 x 4 cm; PVA glue; glue spreaders; pens

Method

This project is fiddly but well worth the end result. It might be best reserved for your most careful and competent groups. Refer to the diagrams closely throughout this activity. You need to be particularly careful with excess glue and to make sure that the ribbons are of equal lengths in order to make the ladder 'fall' properly.

1. Write the letters S, I, N, G, O and D, one on each piece of decorative paper. Make the letters as bold as possible.

2. Line up the pieces of card and, in pencil, label them A, B and C. Turn them over, still in the same order, and label the other sides D, E and F. (Diagram 1)

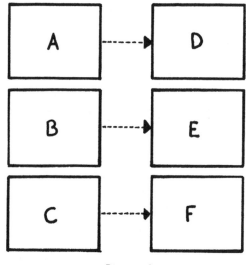

Diagram 1

3. On rectangles A and B, stick a piece of ribbon coming from the centre of the short side of the rectangle on the right. You need to stick down about 1 cm of ribbon; the rest should hang off the side like a tail. (Diagram 2)

4. On the same panels, stick two pieces of ribbon coming from the left-hand side, about 1 cm in from the corners. These rectangles should now have three pieces of ribbon attached, two on the left, and one on the right. Rectangle C should have no ribbon on it yet. (Diagram 2)

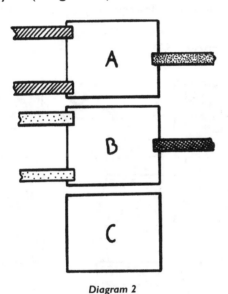

Diagram 2

5. Place panel A on the table with the single ribbon to the right, and fold the two ribbons underneath so that the ends of them show above and below the single ribbon. (Diagram 3)

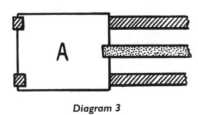

Diagram 3

6. Turn the second panel over so that E is showing and place it on top of A's

single ribbon, with a gap of about 5 mm between the two panels. Lift up the tails of A's double ribbons so that they are on top of panel E and stick them down. Make sure the lengths of ribbon are exactly the same length when you glue them so that the 'ladder' doesn't tilt one way or another. Trim away any excess over 1 cm. Fold A's single ribbon tail back up on to E and glue down. (Diagram 4)

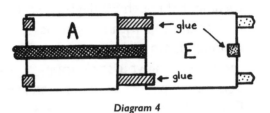

Diagram 4

7. Fold E's single ribbon across E but do not stick it down. (Diagram 5)

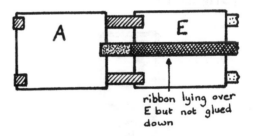

ribbon lying over E but not glued down

Diagram 5

8. If you turn the whole thing over, there should be double ribbons across D and a single ribbon across B *but not stuck to those panels.* You need to be able to slide your decoration under the ribbons later. (Diagram 6)

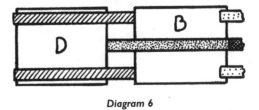

Diagram 6

9. Keeping the panels this way up (D and B showing), place panel F next to B, on top of B's double ribbons, with a gap of about 5 mm between the panels. Stick the ends of the three ribbons on to F. (Diagram 7)

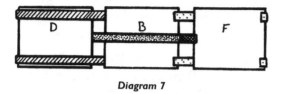

Diagram 7

10. Now turn the whole thing over, turning it through 90 degrees so that A is at the top with the panels running down rather than across. On the side facing you, stick your decorative papers with the letters G, O and D running down. Make sure that you stick them *on top* of the ribbon tails but *under* the full ribbons that run all the way across a panel. (Diagram 8)

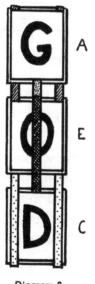

Diagram 8

11. Hold the ladder in one hand by the side edges of the top panel and tilt it backwards 180 degrees. The panels should flip over down the length of the ladder.

12. Place the ladder on the table, with the panel you were holding still at the top. Stick on the letters S, I and N by slipping them under the ribbons as before.

13. Hold up the ladder with SIN showing, and flip the top panel forward. The ladder should now flip down its length and show GOD. Flip the top panel back again, and it shows SIN.

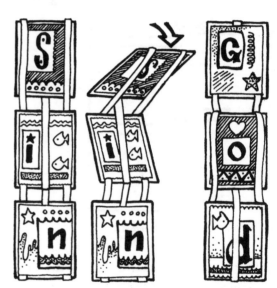

Truth

Logistics

Time – 60 minutes plus drying time; Age – 10 years up; Group – up to 20

Bible link

1 Kings 17:24; Psalm 15; 51:6; 86:11; 101:7; Proverbs 12:17,19; Zechariah 8:16,17; Romans 1:18; 1 Corinthians 13:4–7; 2 Corinthians 4:2; Colossians 3:9,10; 1 John 1:5–10

Introduction

Jesus is the way, truth and life (John 14:6), and if we are to follow him and be like him in all that we say and do, we, too, are called to be truthful. Falsehood and deception are offensive to God, totally contrary to his character, which we are to imitate. When we lie, we dishonour God because we are supposed to reflect his glory.

A more subtle form of lying, of which we're probably all guilty but may not be aware, is the way in which we represent ourselves to others. We all wear disguises, to differing degrees, depending on who we are with or where we are. These disguises or masks can be a form of deceit, hiding our true nature, perhaps because we are worried about what others may think of us. We need to ditch the masks and show who we really are in Christ.

The masks we make in this project are to help us think about the things we seek to hide from others and to challenge us to be more open and truthful in our dealings with others or within ourselves.

You will need

Mounting card; thin card; mask templates; newspaper; white paper; wallpaper paste; paint; masking tape; paste brushes

Method

1. Decide what type of mask you will make – full face or half? – and cut the mounting card to required size and shape, either freehand or using one of the templates from page 61. Note: the mask will be flat, not contoured to fit a face, as this is a reminder, not a mask to be worn. Use thin card to make shapes for any three-dimensional features such as the nose, eyebrows and cheek bones. Stick these on with masking tape. You are making a basic shape which will then be covered with newspaper to give a smoother surface.

2. Tear the newspaper into strips about 2 x 5 cm. Don't be tempted to cut it as the tearing gives ragged edges which blend better.

3. Spread wallpaper paste on the newspaper strips and stick them horizontally over the front of the mask, remembering to overlap. Apply another layer, this time laying the strips vertically, which will help to prevent cracks. If any areas need smoothing, add more paper until the required look is achieved. Now add a final layer of white paper.

4. Leave the masks to dry. This may take a few hours or a few days, depending on the weather and the thickness of the paper layers. Once dry, the masks may be left white, or painted.

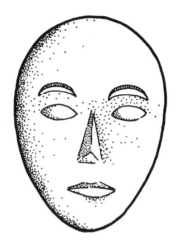

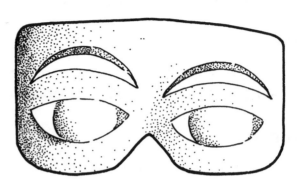

Suffering

Logistics

Time – 10 minutes; Age – 5 years up; Group – up to whole church

Bible link

Pain and suffering: Romans 5: 3–5; 8:28; James 1:2–4; 5:10,11
Suffering as a direct result of the gospel: Acts 14:21,22; Philippians 1:27–30; 1 Peter 2:18–24; 3:13–17; 4:14–19

Introduction

Suffering is always a difficult subject. Christians are frequently asked how they can believe in God when there is so much suffering in the world. We know that God can use the experience of suffering in his people's lives and bring beauty out of it.

This project consists of making a simple paper snowflake. A plain white sheet of paper is marked, folded, cut and has pieces torn away, a bit like our lives. But when the paper is opened out again, the mess of marks and holes has become a beautiful pattern. Remember that, like every snowflake, you are unique and precious to God.

You will need

A circle of white paper per person – see template on page 62; scissors

Method

1. Fold the circle along the dotted lines, so that you end up with a roughly triangular shape.

2. Cut away pieces from the edges, being careful not to cut all the way from one edge to the other.

3. Unfold the circle, and you will have a snowflake shape.

Alternative idea

If you are doing this with a church congregation, why not put large pieces of dark paper on the wall? Play some reflective music and encourage people to come and offer up their suffering or others' suffering to God by sticking their snowflakes on the dark background. You will end up with a huge visual aid to help you, as you offer these situations up to God corporately.

Fruit of the Spirit

Logistics

Time – 60 minutes; Age – teens up; Group – up to 15

Bible link

Matthew 7:15–20; 12:33–37; John 15:16; Galatians 5:22,23

Introduction

When a person becomes a Christian, a change is seen in their life through the work of the Holy Spirit. A good tree produces good fruit (Matthew 7:18) and the fruit is seen by all. Our friends and family should notice a change in us, and an increase in those qualities spoken of in Galatians 5: 22,23 – the fruit of the Spirit. As we have faith and allow the Spirit to work on us, by God's grace we increase in these desirable qualities.

This project involves making a bowl of fruit, to remind us of the qualities that we should increasingly display as we grow in the fruit of the Spirit.

You will need

Paper; scissors; light card; pens for decorating; bowl and fruit templates from pages 63–64.

Method

Preparation: photocopy one bowl template from page 63 on paper and one set of fruit templates from page 64 per person on light card. Allow a couple of spare bowl templates for the group, in case of mishaps.

1. To make the bowl, with the plain side of the paper facing you, fold in the corners to make crease lines along the lines of the central square. Unfold again. (Diagram 1)

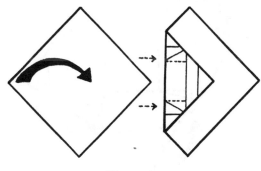

Diagram 1

2. Fold the paper in half vertically and unfold it. Try to avoid folding too heavily in the central square. (Diagram 2)

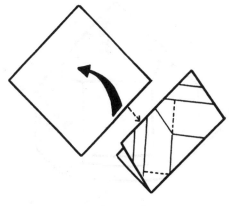

Diagram 2

3. Now fold the paper in half horizontally, again avoiding folding too heavily in the central square. There should now be folds along the solid lines coming from the corners of the central square.

4. Turn the paper over so that all the black lines are now facing you.

5. Fold the folds just made across, so that the solid line coming from the corner of the inner square meets the dotted line and crease. (Diagram 3) This should push the corners of the central square up towards you, *not* down towards the table.

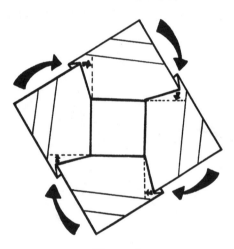

Diagram 3

6. Fold the corners down twice at the solid lines. This should lock the other folds in place. (Diagram 4)

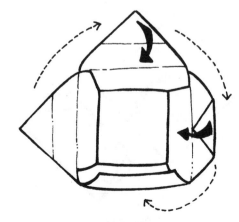

Diagram 4

7. Turn the finished bowl over. Any black fold lines should be on the outside of the bowl.

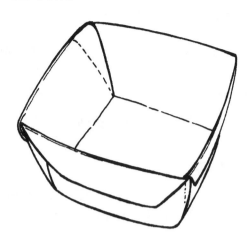

8. Cut out and decorate the fruit templates. Write one of the names of the fruit of the Spirit – love, joy, peace, patience, kindness, goodness, faithfulness, gentleness, self control – on each.

9. Place the fruit in the bowl.

Alternative idea

Adapt this project to help you look at the gifts of the Spirit, too, by making a bag of tools. Photocopy the bag and tools templates on pages 65–66 on card and give each person one bag and several tools.

Decorate the bag on the plain side and follow the instructions on the template for folding and gluing. Punch the marked holes and thread string or ribbon through them to form handles. Write the names of the various gifts of the Spirit on the tools and place them in the bag.

Good Friday – Atonement

Logistics

Time – depends on group size; Age – any; Group – up to full church

Bible link

Leviticus 16:1–22; Isaiah 53:4–6; Mark 15:21–39 and parallels; Romans 3:21–26; 5:15–17; 2 Corinthians 5:21; Colossians 1:19–23; 2:9–14

Introduction

In the Old Testament, sin is dealt with by the offering of a blood sacrifice. In the New Testament, we see that a sacrifice is still required but it is the sacrifice of Christ in our place. Good Friday saw the perfect atonement for our sins, and therefore the abolition of any further need for blood sacrifice. The perfect sacrifice had been made once-for-all on the cross.

In this project, a cross is made of handprints. This is symbolic of acknowledging our hand in Jesus' death, admitting that we are responsible for that. We also place our handprints upon the cross as an echo of the Jewish priest laying his hands on the scapegoat on the Day of Atonement (Leviticus 16:20–22).

You will need

A piece of paper with enough room for handprints of the entire group, or several large pieces which can be assembled into a cross; poster paint; paintbrushes; bowls of water; old towels

Method

1. Sketch a rough outline of a cross on the paper.

2. Each person needs to cover his palm and fingers with paint then print them on the cross.

3. Wash hands in bowl of water and dry on old towels. This is symbolic of the washing away of our sin through Jesus' death for us.

If you're doing this with large numbers, have several stations at which hands can be painted and washed, and print hands onto rectangular sheets of paper. These can then be assembled at the front of the church into a huge cross shape.

Covenant

Logistics

Time – 30 minutes; Age – 10 years up; Group – up to 20

Bible link

Genesis 9:8–17; 17:1–21; Exodus 34:10–28; 1 Samuel 18:1–4; Isaiah 24:5; Hebrews 8:6–13; 12:18–24

Introduction

A covenant between God and man is a legal agreement between unequal parties which lays down conditions for the relationship between those parties. The inequity here also means that man cannot negotiate the terms.

Probably the best-known covenant is the new covenant of grace whereby Jesus, as mediator, fulfilled the conditions for us to be reconciled to God. We then need to have faith and obedience to participate in the covenant and receive the promised blessing – eternal life. The sign and seal of entering into this covenant is baptism in the name of Jesus. As we continue living in this covenant, we should see an increasing obedience to God in our life.

For this project we will make scrolls and write on them the conditions, requirements and blessing of the covenant of grace, putting in our own names as the parties involved in this covenant with God.

You will need

Sheets of A4 paper; red ribbon – about 0.5 m per person; pens; scrap paper; inkpad

Method

1. On the scrap paper, plan how you will arrange the wording on your scroll. Remember, it needs to include the following: the names of the two parties involved in the agreement; the requirement – death for sin, which Jesus takes on for us; conditions for participation – repentance and faith; the promise from God – eternal life. The wording might be something like that illustrated on the next page.

2. Once you have worked out the layout to your satisfaction, write it on the sheet of A4. You could decorate it with a seal, as in a legal document, or use an inkpad to make your thumbprint at the bottom to show you are willing to fulfil the conditions for participation.

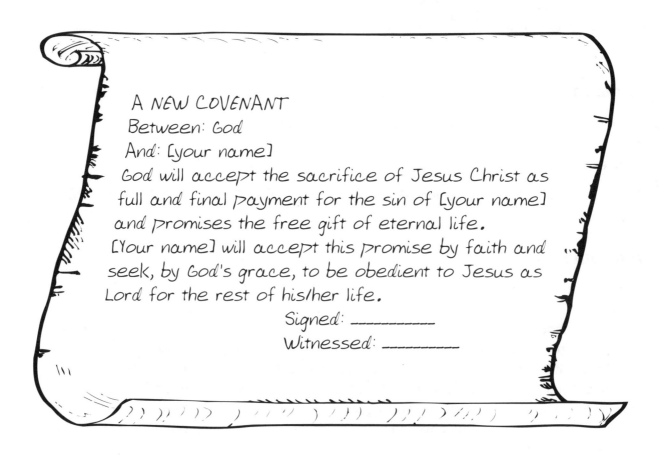

A NEW COVENANT

Between: God

And: [your name]

God will accept the sacrifice of Jesus Christ as full and final payment for the sin of [your name] and promises the free gift of eternal life.

[Your name] will accept this promise by faith and seek, by God's grace, to be obedient to Jesus as Lord for the rest of his/her life.

Signed: _____

Witnessed: _____

3. When the scroll is finished, roll it up, and tie with the red ribbon.

If you're doing this with large numbers in church, you could type the wording of the document beforehand and photocopy one for each member of the congregation. Church members could then simply fill in their names, decorate and sign the scrolls.

Adoption

Logistics

Time – 30 minutes; Age – 10 years up; Group – up to 20

Bible link

1 Kings 21:8; Esther 3:12; 8:7,8; Daniel 6:16–18; Romans 8:14–17; 2 Corinthians 1:21,22; Galatians 3:23 – 4:7; Ephesians 4:30; Revelation 7:2–5 – sealed against separation from God; Revelation 14:1

Introduction

Being adopted by God means being made a member of his family, with all the benefits which that entails. We are marked as belonging to the Father, and have assurance from the Spirit that we are his, although we wait to receive our inheritance in heaven (1 Peter 1:4) and our resurrection bodies when Christ returns.

It is this idea of being marked as God's child that provides the basis for this project. We are sealed by the Spirit, and the Greek word used in several of the verses above means 'to seal'; 'to mark something to show possession, authority, security, or identity'. We are going to make a seal to remind us that we belong to God, and that because of the seal he places upon us, we will be clearly shown to be his.

You will need

Polymer clay (available from craft shops and some toy shops); a rolling pin or bottle to flatten the clay; various mark-making tools – pens, wire, keys, bottle tops, anything which can make an interesting impression on the clay; old newspapers or scrap card; cornflour; plasticine or sealing wax on which to print your seal

Method

1. Give everyone a piece of clay. About 15 g will be sufficient for each person.

2. Following the manufacturer's instructions, soften the clay until it is ready to use. Form a ball or oval shape then flatten the clay on the newspapers or card, using the rolling pin or bottle. If the clay is a bit sticky, put cornflour on your hands and on the newspapers while you work it. Your seal should be approximately 5 mm thick.

3. Using whichever instruments you choose, make marks in the clay. You could write a word, remembering to reverse it so that the image is the right way round when printed, or you could just make a pattern. Keep the surface as flat as possible. Trim the edges of your seal if you wish to create a regular shape, such as a square or triangle.

4. Bake the clay seal, following the instructions on the packet.

5. Now try your seal out by making an impression in some plasticine or in a large blob of sealing wax.

Pentecost

Logistics

Time – 30 minutes; Age – 10 years up; Group – up to 10

Bible link

Acts 2

Introduction

What a change came about in the disciples when they were filled with the Holy Spirit at Pentecost! They had previously been believers and witnesses, but now they had a boldness and a visibly different way of living. The Holy Spirit shone through their words and deeds in a way apparent to all.

We are told that tongues of fire appeared and rested on the disciples. The illustrated Bible I had as a child included a lovely picture of this event which made me think of the disciples as candles. That's a good visual symbol of our call to live as light in the world, so we are going to make candles.

If you have ever watched a thick candle burn down, you will have noticed that as the flame goes below the surface of the candle, it makes the whole candle glow from within. This is a good picture of us when we are filled with the Holy Spirit. Candles can look good, but until they are lit, they are lifeless.

You will need

Candle wax (available from craft shops or www.uk.opitec.com); wick; wax crayons; a sharp knife; a glass for each person – these can be bought in charity shops, or you might ask each person to bring one. (Smaller thicker glasses are good, as they take less wax.); old saucepans of varied sizes; a cooker; pencils; scissors

Method

1. Cut a piece of wick, the height of the glass plus 5 cm. Tie one end of the wick around a pencil and balance the pencil on top of the glass, the wick reaching to the bottom.

2. Decide whether you want your candle all one colour or in stripes. If you require stripes, do not melt all the wax at once, as you will want to colour it in several batches.

3. Place some wax, with some wax crayon to colour it, in an old saucepan inside a saucepan of water. Heat over a gentle heat, watching it all the time.

4. When the wax has melted, pour it into each glass. You can make angled stripes by tipping the glass slightly as you allow the wax to set.

5. While each layer is solidifying, repeat steps 3 and 4 until everyone has a candle in a glass.

6. Untie the pencil from the end of the wick and trim the wick to about 1 cm.

7. Do not dispose of candle wax down the sink as it will solidify and block the drain. Pour any left-over wax into a bowl of cold water. It will harden and you can then lift it out and dispose of it in a bin or keep it to melt down again another time.

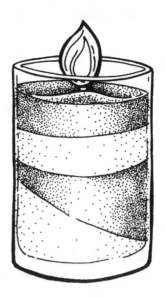

Thanksgiving

Logistics

Time – 30 minutes; Age – 5 years up; Group – up to 20

Bible link

1 Chronicles 16:34; Psalm 50:23; Psalm 118:21; Philippians 4:4–7; Colossians 3:17; 1 Thessalonians 5:16–18

Introduction

Psalm 50 says that if we offer thanksgiving, we honour God. We are told to offer up thanks whatever our circumstances may be. Sometimes we feel 'down', and not at all like giving thanks. At times like this, it is good to look back at what God has already done for us and give thanks for that. We quickly come back to feeling more grateful.

To help us remember what God has done for us, we are going to make a 'Thank You' card for God.

You will need

Card; pens; materials for decoration – coloured paper, felt-tips, punches, rubber stamps etc; glue; scissors

Method

1. Decorate your chosen card in any way you wish. Try – stamping, cutting out shapes and sticking them on the card, drawing patterns – use your imagination.

2. Now turn your attention to the inside. What are you thankful for? What has God done for you? Write it inside. If you're working with young children, they might like to draw a picture of what they'd like to thank God for. Next time life seems awful, open the card, and remember how much we have to thank God for.

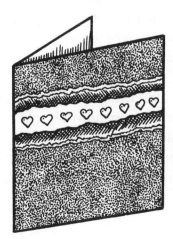  

Fruitfulness

Logistics

Time – 60 minutes; Age – 14 years up; Group – up to 10

Bible link

Psalm 1:1–3; John 15:1–11; Romans 7:4; Galatians 5:22–26; Colossians 1:9,10

Introduction

All through the Bible, there are references to fruit and fruitfulness. In Genesis, Adam and Eve are told to be fruitful and multiply. In the New Testament, *we* are asked to be fruitful – to display the characteristics of Christ and to spread the message of the gospel, thus producing a crop 30, 60 or 100 times greater than that which was sown.

Sowing a crop means starting with a little and turning it into much more. This book we are about to make looks small on the outside but is surprisingly large when opened out.

You will need

Thick card; paper – plain and decorative; pens; PVA glue; glue spreaders; scissors

Method

1. Give each person two pieces of card 5 x 5 cm. These will form the book covers.

2. Using some decorative paper, cut out two squares slightly larger than the card – enough to fold over and glue on the inside. Apply glue to one side of the card and stick it to the paper. Fold over the edges – corners first looks neater – and glue it down.

3. Cut out a square of plain paper 10 x 10 cm. Fold it in half edge to edge, open it out, then fold it in half the other way so that the opened-out paper is marked into squares. Now turn the paper over and fold it in half corner to corner. (Diagram 1)

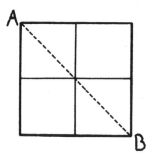

Diagram 1

4. Turn the paper over again and place it on the table so the corner to corner fold runs vertically from top to bottom, and the fold forms a peak rather than a valley. Write Matthew 13:3b–8 – either in full, paraphrased or just the reference – on this side of the paper.

5. Fold the corners in towards each other. The corner-to-corner fold should fold in neatly so that you are left with a square the same size as the covers you made earlier. (Diagram 2)

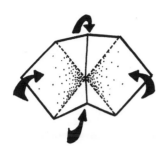

Diagram 2

6. Glue the folded paper on the covers so that when the covers are opened, the paper can be opened out to its original size – four times the size of the covers.

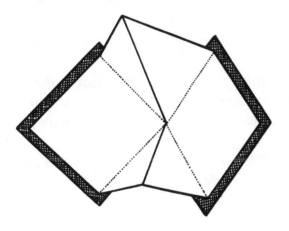

Alternative idea

Use this activity to think about the theme of the Kingdom of Heaven, growing from small beginnings.

Bible link: Matthew 13:31,32; 17:20,21; 21:18–22; 25:14–30; Mark 4:1–9; 4:30–32; Luke 13:18,19

Light

Logistics

Time – 30 minutes; Age – 10 years up; Group – up to 15

Bible link

Genesis 1:3–5; 2 Samuel 22:29; Isaiah 9:2; Matthew 5:14–16; 6:22,23; John 1:1–13; 3:16–23; 8:12; 11:9,10; 12:35,36,46; Revelation 22:5

Introduction

In the beginning God separated the light and the darkness from each other. From that time on, light has been associated with God – he is in the pillar of fire in the wilderness; many of the biblical visions of God include references to the light that surrounds him; Jesus calls himself the light of the world; he even tells us that *we*, as his children, are the light of the world.

This project is to make a tea-light shade. Without the light behind it, the shade is dull but once the candle is placed inside, the true beauty of the shade shows up. Similarly, the light of the Holy Spirit in us should be visible to others, radiating something of God's character.

'People are like stained glass windows. They sparkle and shine when the sun is out but when the darkness sets in, their true beauty is revealed only if there is a light from within.'
Elizabeth Kübler-Ross

You will need

A4 thin card; tissue paper in different colours; PVA glue; glue spreaders; tea-lights; scissors; stapler (optional)

Method

1. Cut the A4 card into strips, 3 cm wide. Each person will need four strips.

2. Place two strips about 15 cm apart. Cut the other two strips into shorter even lengths and stick as many as necessary between the two long strips to keep them evenly spaced and stop the tissue paper sagging. Tear or cut some strips of tissue paper and stick them in the gaps between the card strips until you have a rectangle with card at top and bottom and tissue in the middle.

3. Bend the card round until the ends join, and glue or staple the ends together.

4. Place the shade over a lit tea-light and see how the colours glow.

TAKE CARE WITH LIT CANDLES

Sacrifice

Logistics

Time – 30 minutes plus drying time; Age – 5 years up; Group – up to 20

Bible link

Exodus 30:22–38; Psalm 141:2; Romans 12:1,2; Ephesians 5:1,2; Hebrews 13:14–16; Revelation 8:4

Introduction

In the temple, offerings were made to God and fragrant incense was burnt, its scent mingling with the smell of the burning sacrifice. Our prayers and loving actions now rise as a fragrant offering to God since Jesus has made the perfect blood sacrifice.

This project is to make a pomander, to remind us that our offerings are a pleasing fragrance to God.

You will need

An orange and a paper bag per person; cloves; cinnamon; orris root powder (optional); ribbon; sticky tape; toothpicks

Method

1. Wrap sticky tape twice around the orange from top to bottom, so that the orange has four 'segments'. This is where the ribbon will go.

2. Using toothpicks, make holes all over the orange. Push the cloves into the holes, taking care not to break them.

3. In a paper bag, mix equal amounts of cinnamon with orris root powder (approx 1 tsp each), toss the orange in, and shake it until coated with powder.

4. Leave the orange in the bag for a couple of weeks, in a warm dry place such as an airing cupboard.

5. Remove the orange from the bag, peel off the sticky tape, and tie on the ribbon in its place, making a loop at the top so that you can hang up the pomander.

Christmas

Logistics

Time – 5 to 30 minutes; Age – all ages; Group – up to whole church.

Bible link

Matthew 1:18 – 2:12; Luke 2:1–20; John 3:16; Ephesians 2:8; 1 Peter 4:10

Introduction

Christmas is a time of giving. We give presents to those we love in remembrance that the Father made the gift of his Son to us. So what gift will you lay at God's feet this year? Your finances? The use of your house? Your organisational skills? Make God a gift of something he has given you this year.

You will need

Pieces of thin card; box template from page 59; slips of paper; pens; decorative paper; sticky tape; scissors; PVA glue; glue spreaders

Method

1. Photocopy the small box template on thin card, one per person.

2. Cut out the template.

3. Fold the box along the lines shown and glue the tabs as marked.

4. Now write on a slip of paper what you are going to give to God this year. Put the paper in the box.

5. Wrap the box as a gift. Keep it in a safe place and next Christmas, open the gift to remind yourself of what you gave to God. See what he did with it during the year.

Lent

Logistics

Time – 30 minutes; Age – teens up; Group – up to 15

Bible link

Thinking about Lent: Matthew 6:16–18; Luke 4:1–13
Treasuring God's Word: Deuteronomy 11:18,19; Psalm 77:11,12; Psalm 119; Psalm 143:5; Luke 2:19

Introduction

What does Lent suggest to you? Deprivation? A time of giving things up? No chocolate? Why not make this year different and take something up for Lent? Keep a journal. Go on – it's only for 47 days. Use the time leading up to the principal festival of the Christian year to improve your relationship with God by giving up a little time each day to reflect on God's Word and make a record of the things that strike you from your study.

To encourage you to keep going, make a journal in which you can write your musings – something you'll want to use and keep.

You will need

47 pieces of A5 paper per person; 1 piece of A5 thick (mounting) card per person; 1 piece of A5 thin card per person; a hole punch; ribbon or string; pens etc, for decorating

Method

1. Stack the paper and card with the thick card at the bottom and the thin card at the top. Arrange them so the shorter ends are at the side (landscape orientation).

2. Punch two holes in the left-hand side of the stack. These are for the ribbon or string, so make sure they line up.

3. Decorate the thin card cover by drawing, painting, or sticking on pictures.

4. Thread ribbon or string through the holes and tie it in a firm double bow. Carefully score the card cover next to the holes so it will open and the book can lie flat.

5. Write the dates of Lent and Holy Week, one on each page.

6. *Important* – write in the book every day during Lent. What should you write? Why not work through a Bible guide for 40 days during Lent – something like *The Purpose Driven Life* or *The Essential 100* paperback (*Share the Light* edition, Scripture Union). Or use any other set of Bible readings – just something on which to focus your thoughts and Bible exploration. Use the journal to record new things learnt, your feelings about what the Bible says, reflections on your walk with God. If you have given something up for Lent, why not track how you've coped without it? How has its absence changed the way you've responded to God?

The big picture

Logistics

Time – 10–60 minutes; Age – all; Group – up to whole church

Bible link

2 Kings 19:25,26; Job 23:8–10; Jeremiah 29:10–14; 1 Corinthians 13:8–12

Introduction

Have there been times in your life when you have wondered what on earth is going on, only to look back on those times later and see how the Lord moved? From close up, we see the small picture. God sees the big picture, from a heavenly perspective.

This project involves making a mosaic. All the small pieces fit together to make a picture which we can only see fully when everything is slotted into place.

You will need

A sheet of paper; very small squares of paper of different colours; PVA glue; glue spreaders; pencils; scrap paper; pens (optional)

Method

1. Sketch a picture on the paper, keeping it simple. Try it out on scrap paper first if you wish. Abstract patterns can look very effective.

2. Stick on squares of coloured paper to make the picture.

Alternative ideas

If you are using this in a 'whole church' setting, have someone plan a picture, and mark each area with the colour it needs to be. Each person in the congregation is then given a coloured square, puts his or her name on it, then sticks it to the picture.

With large groups, how about having several pieces of paper which are different sections that will make up a whole picture when put together? Place these at different stations around the church, then, at the end of the activity, piece them together at the front. The names on the squares show how everyone plays a part in making up the big picture.

Worship (1)

Worship (2)

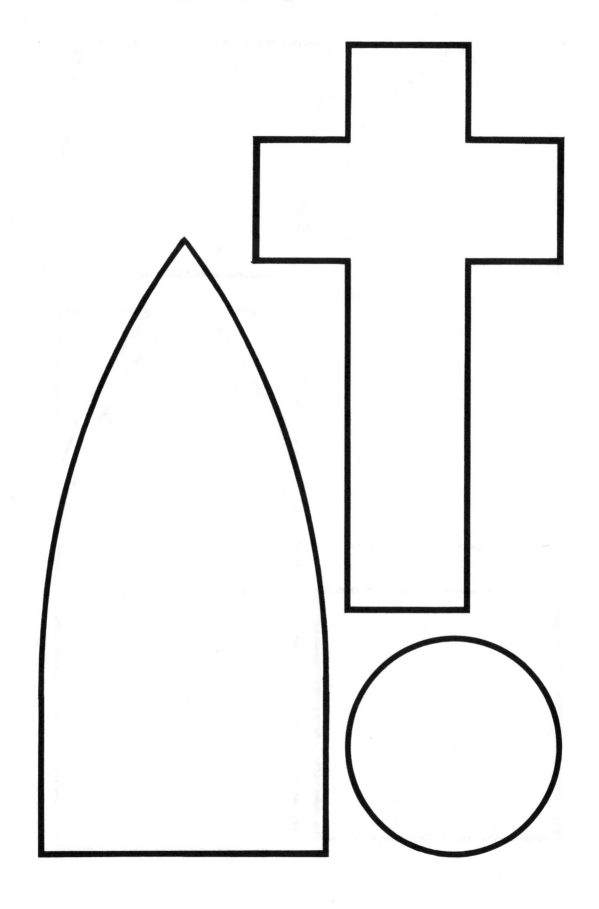

Reconciliation/Christmas

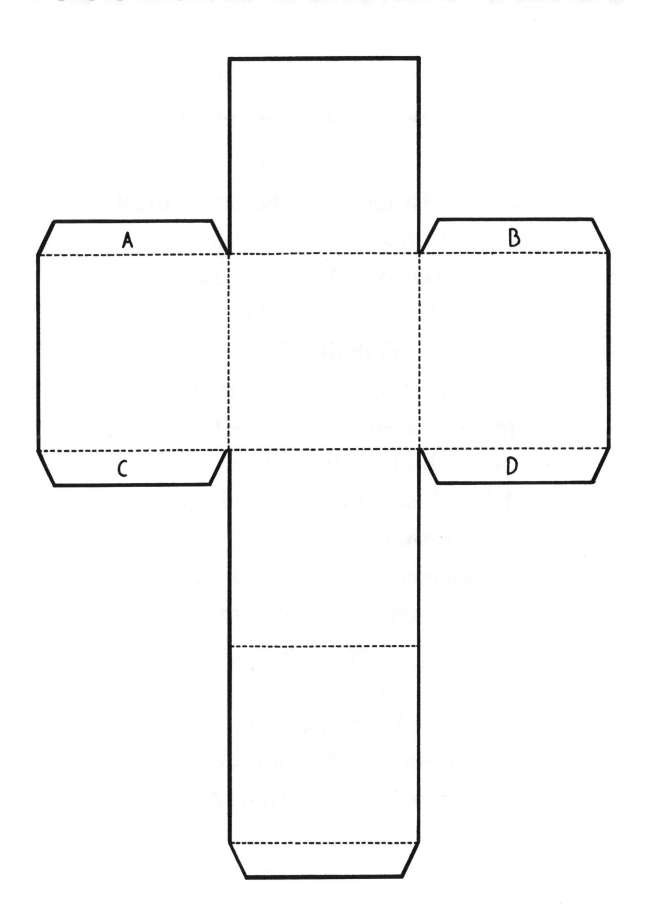

Some names of God

Abir – Mighty One

Adonai – Lord

El-Elohe-Israel – God, the God of Israel

El-Elyon – God Most High

El-Olam – Everlasting God

El Shaddai – Almighty God

Elohim – God

Emmanuel – God with us

Jehovah-jireh – the Lord will provide

Jehovah-nissi – the Lord, my banner

Jehovah-shalom – the Lord is peace

Jehovah-shammah – the Lord is there

Jehovah-tsidkenu – the Lord our righteousness

Jehovah-sebaoth – the Lord of hosts

King of Kings

Lion of Judah

Lord of Lords

Messiah – Anointed One

Yahweh (Jehovah) – I AM

Truth

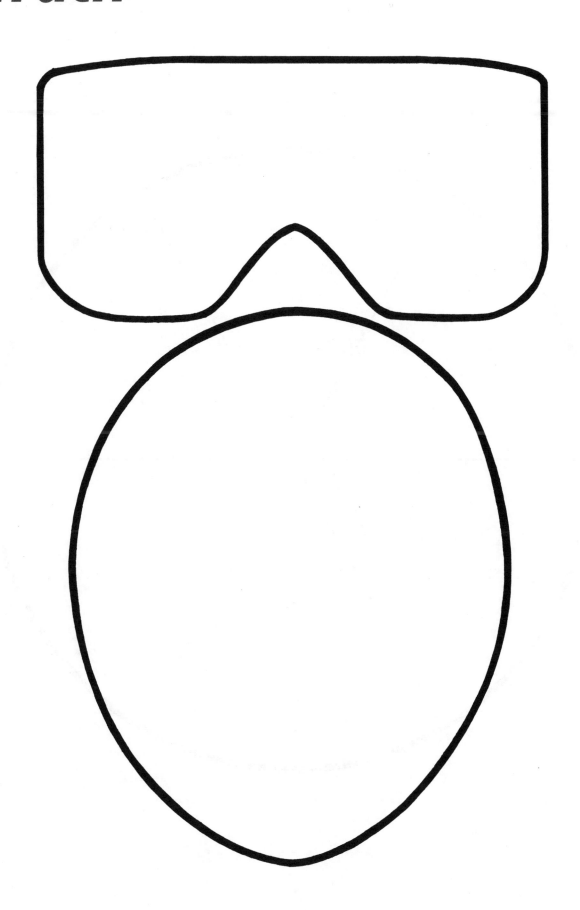

Suffering

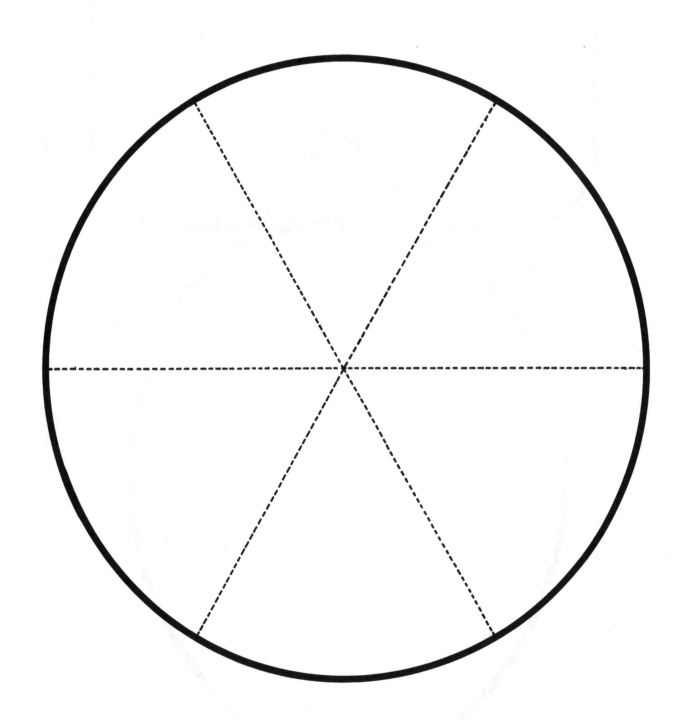

Fruit of the Spirit (1)

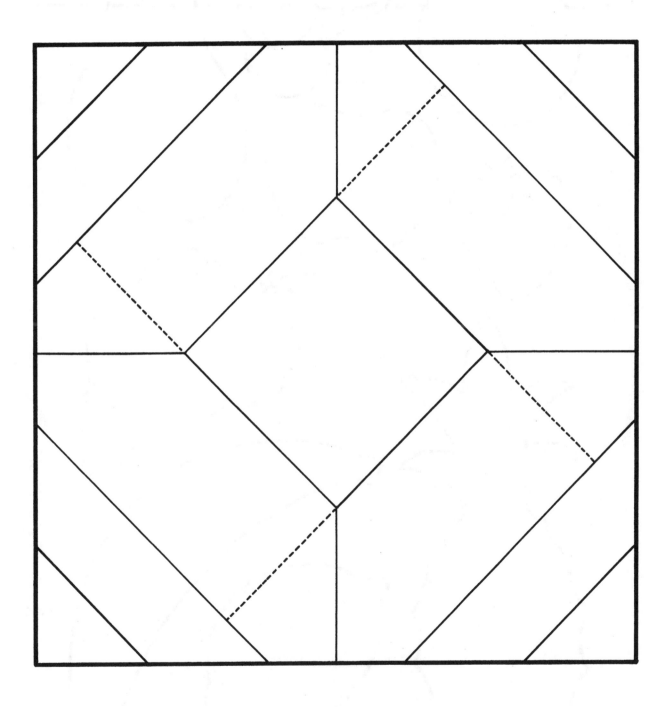

Fruit of the Spirit (2)

Spiritual Gifts (1)

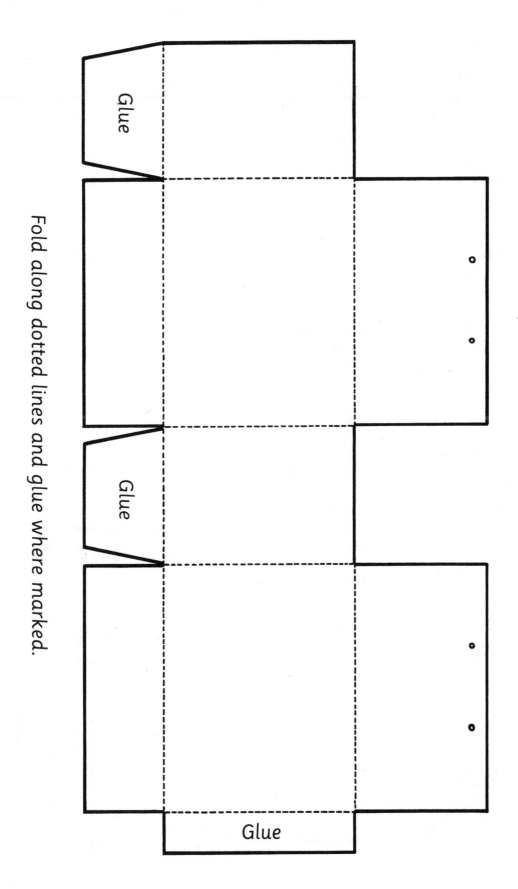

Glue

Fold along dotted lines and glue where marked.

Glue

Glue

Spiritual Gifts (2)

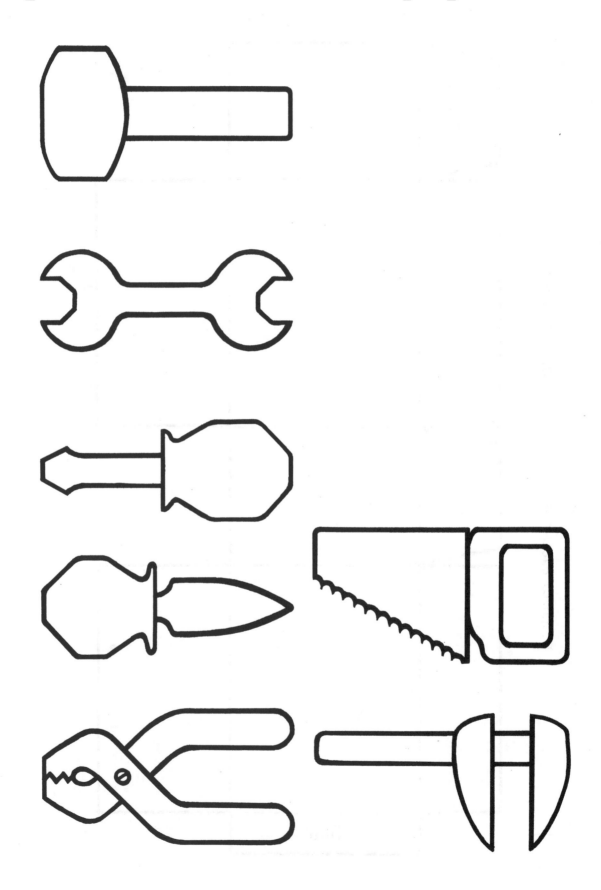

Bible index

Theme index

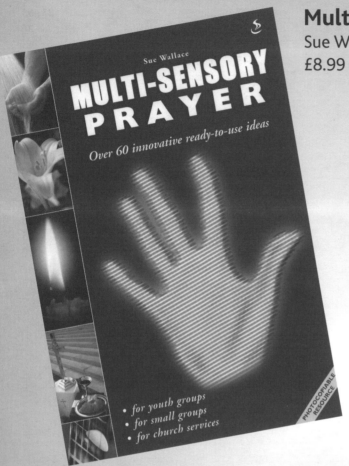

Available Spring 2005

Faith Shapers

25 crafts with a message for kids' groups

Nadia Herbert

Looking for engaging, hands-on activities for 8–11s? Faith Shapers provides you with 25 themed craft ideas and top tips for building relationships as you have fun.

Each craft has:

- *A suggested Bible passage*

- *Ideas for engaging children in informal discussion on the theme*

- *A related prayer idea*

Available from your local Christian bookshop or
Scripture Union Mail Order, PO Box 5148, Milton Keynes MLO, MK2 2YX

Tel: 0845 070 6006 Fax: 01908 856020

www.scriptureunion.org.uk